a year in the life of north cornwall rob beighton

FRANCES LINCOLN

a year in the life of north cornwall rob beighton

Frances Lincoln Limited
4 Torriano Mews
Torriano Avenue
London NW5 2RZ
www.franceslincoln.com

Title page Sandy mouth.

contents

a year in the life of north cornwall

Cornwall, England's most westerly county, remains a haven of sanity in the headlong rush of the 21st century. As you enter Cornwall at Plymouth, where the highway crosses the river Tamar from Devon, there's a sense of moving into the unknown; maybe it is the fact of crossing the water to arrive here that from now on, as you travel westwards, you feel as if you are on an island, set apart from the normal flow of life. This book is a visual and perhaps romantic view of the northern aspect of the peninsula, a celebration of the region through the seasons, of the wild and rugged coast between Marsland mouth in the northeast to Land's End at the south-western tip and of the equally rugged uplands of Penwith and Bodmin moor. It is a sampling of the character of the area, rather than a comprehensive guide.

the hand of man

Left Crackington Haven, a trickle of houses at the mouth of a fine wooded valley, seen across Bray's point.

Right The little town of Port Isaac crowding almost to the cliff's edge.

Left Golitha falls in the headwaters of the Fowey river as rain water spills from Bodmin Moor a few miles away. Early autumn hangs in the air.

unspoilt nature

Right Looking across the headland of Porthmissen Bridge, near Trevone, towards Gunver Head on a spring evening after a heavy storm.

Much of the charm of Cornwall lies in the fine balance between the unspoilt qualities of the landscape and the particular character that has been laid on it by the acts of man throughout many centuries. The earliest occupation of the region is believed to be by the Neolithic Beaker people of the stone age. Four thousand years ago in the Megalithic period men were erecting stone posts and circles and constructing stone chambers to bury the dead. This period gave way to the Bronze age where copper and tin, the two constituents of the metallic alloy, bronze, were to be found here at the surface of the land. In the region of 550 BC Celtic tribes invaded Britain, bringing with them the knowledge of working iron. As with all the western peninsulas of Britain, the Celtic influence remained strong for many centuries, with the last remnants of the living language dying out in Cornwall in the 1800s. Mining for copper and tin, rather than simply finding the metals in rivers, began in the northern parts of the county in the 1500s, reaching a high level of development in the 1700s with Richard Trevithick's innovative use of coal and steam power for stationary engines and for locomotives. In the 1800s the passenger railways established throughout Britain allowed ordinary people the freedom of travel previously only available to the rich. Cornwall began to be visited by increasing numbers of people who wished to enjoy the pleasure of its favoured mild climate on its many fine beaches. Today it is amongst the country's best loved holiday destinations, with countless thousands arriving to sample the unique atmosphere, as well as the pasties and clotted cream. The other main traditional industry, fishing, is now secondary to tourism.

Butter Hole near Stepper Point, Padstow, after a period of heavy weather in spring. A day of drama on land and sea.

winter

Winter, a time for most of nature to hibernate and allow energies to renew for the next year. Clear skies and reduced hours of daylight bring falling temperatures and the visual delight of sparkles of frost on leaves; late risers will miss this gift of nature as the sun quickly turns it back into water. In this mellow corner of the British Isles snow is seldom seen, except on the high ground of Bodmin moor.

Right Frosted leaves of blackberry.

Next page Early morning frost and mist lie in a valley near Wadebridge in early winter.

Previous page A storm explodes the ocean against the cliffs near Carnweather Point, Polzeath.

Above Dartmoor ponies spend the winter grazing the clifftop pastures near Port Quin.

18

Above right Sunset from Pendeen watch.

Next page Dawn near Wadebridge.

19

This page Quartz streaked rock at Yeol mouth, near Morwenstow.

Opposite page Horse on Bodmin moor at sunset.

On the Saint's Way above Little Petherick creek, Padstow, in late winter. A fine and easy walk.

This page The Rumps, near Polzeath, in a late winter storm.

Next page Winter moonlight, Wadebridge.

27

Cornwall is rich in evidence of the past. Stone circles, standing stones and burial chambers, legacies of the ancient occupation of the region, are to be found in the higher, more remote parts of the peninsula, particularly on Bodmin moor and in large numbers on the peninsula of west Penwith, between St Ives and Land's End. Promontory forts, small fortified headlands into the sea, can be found in a number of places, such as Rumps point near Padstow. The dramatic cliff top castle at Tintagel is associated with the legend of King Arthur, being where he is held to have spent his early years. However, evidence suggests that it was built in the mid-twelfth century in the reign of Reginald, Earl of Cornwall. Inscribed stone crosses and posts can be seen on roadsides throughout the county.

Opposite page The Hurlers, three Bronze Age stone circles near Minions on Bodmin moor.

Above Trippet stones, a Bronze Age stone circle on Hawkstor downs, Bodmin moor.

Bottom left King Doniert's stone near St Cleer, Bodmin moor, dates from the ninth century.

Bottom right Three Holes Cross, near Wadebridge.

Previous page Tintagel Head, with its spectacular castle poised above the ocean.

Left Ponies sheltering from the snow below Rough Tor, on the north edge of Bodmin Moor.

Opposite Bodmin Moor ponies are a distinct wild breed.

Bodmin Moor is a wild area of upland lying to the south-east of Camelford and rising to the modest height of 420 metres on the rocky outcrop of Brown Willy. A mysterious and elemental place of bogs and granite, cut by frothing streams and threaded by ancient tracks. Days spent here feel from another time; with the skylark rising into a clear June sky there is a rare sense of peace. In winter with snow on the ground or with mist wreathing the rocky tors the story is altogether more severe. Farms shelter in the wooded hollows that wind down to the edge of the moor.

bodmin moor

Following page Rough Tor in winter.

spring

Spring arrives early in this most westerly part of England, with a great wealth of wild flowers growing in the wooded valleys. In this small wood lies a rich profusion of flowers which thrive in the shelter of oak and sycamore trees. Before the trees leaf, sunlight is able to warm the woodland floor, encouraging the bulbs of bluebell to start their year. Later in the season, in May or June, the flowers benefit from the shelter of the canopy of leaves to keep off the heat of the sun.

Spring flowers alongside the Camel Trail, near Wadebridge.

Right and below Spring flowers, bluebell and wild garlic, in Hustyns wood, near Burlawn, Wadebridge.

Left Common fern, with bluebells.

Below Herb Robert.

Above Stone stile near Wenford bridge, a characteristic feature of Cornwall's field boundaries.

Below and right Wild garlic in Hustyn's wood.

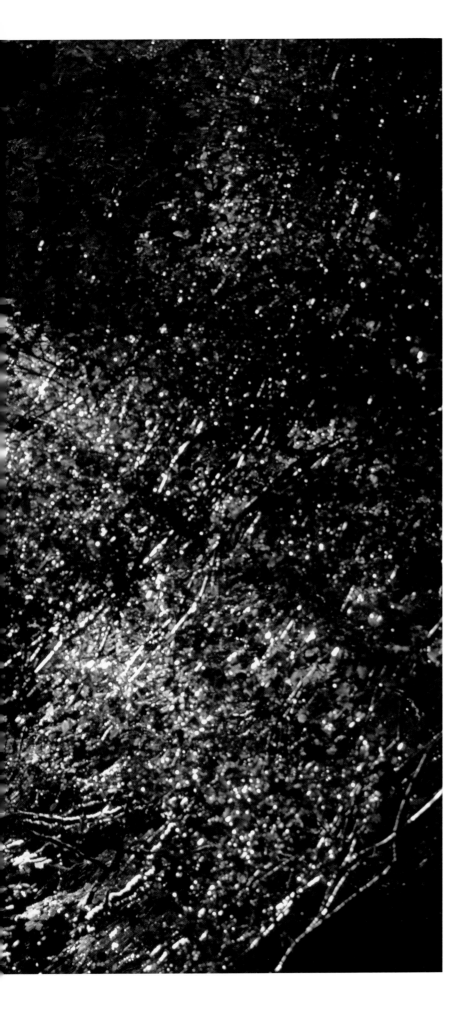

Left Spring sunlight lights up beech trees near Golitha falls, Bodmin.

Below Wood anemone.

Spring flowers

Opposite page clockwise Wild apple blossom, squill, foxglove, wild rose, dog daisy, centaury.

This page Wild iris and buttercup near Port Isaac.

Sunset stains the ocean off Stowe cliffs to the
north of Bude. Sea pink flowers in profusion here.

Opposite Sea pink, or thrift as it is also known, grows in great carpets in many places along Cornwall's coast, as here near Godrevy point.

Below Goats live wild on the cliff top near Lower Sharpnose point.

Right One man and his dog, fishing in the Fowey river below Golitha falls, to the south-west of Bodmin moor.

Next page Sunset colours the sky above the Padstow estuary at the mouth of the river Camel.

mining

Opposite Perched on the brink of the ocean, Botallack mine buildings are a striking legacy of former times. Tin has been extracted from the rocks along Cornwall's coast for 3000 years.

Below lower The characteristic construction of the mine chimney, with stone below and brick above, seen here at Levant.

Below upper Shaft winding gear at Levant.

the coast path

The Cornish coast path is a continuous waymarked walking path which extends for 300 miles from the northern border with Devon at Marsland mouth to the southern border near Plymouth, although for this book we are looking at the northern section as far as Land's End. It is part of the South West Coast Path, a right of way across coastal land, some of which is private, some owned by the National Trust and running through Somerset, north Devon, Cornwall, south Devon and Dorset. The landscape is immensely varied with beaches and coves of golden sand, curious little fishing villages, woodlands of twisted, wind blown trees and rugged, rocky cliffs, rising to almost 250 metres to the south of Crackington haven; a wonderland of largely unspoilt nature.

Left Looking across Dinas head to Trevose head light house.

Below One of the many flights of wooden steps on the wonderful stretch of the coast path to the north of Trebarwith.

There is a magnificent flavour to a walk along a section of the path, of cultivated farmland on the one hand and the sense of unspoilt wilderness o the ever present ocean on the other. River valleys frequently intersect the coast, where pretty tumbles of houses crowd around a fishing harbour On a multi-day walk, these villages appear as oases in the solitude of the path, giving a very different sense to that when they are reached by car

Opposite Early morning on the path near Portreath, Camborne in early spring mist.

Below Descending from Varley head towards Port Quin, a wild and ruggedly undulating stretch.

summer

Clear, bright blue skies; towering masses of shining white fair weather cumulus clouds; gentle breezes; seemingly endless hours of daylight; symbols of summer days. Cornwall lies in the North Atlantic Drift, the Gulf Stream, ànd has a latitude similar to that of northern France so summer here has real heat, with days hot enough to lounge for hours on beaches.

Opposite Fair summer weather cumulus cloud near Camelford.

Following page Sunset at Rumps beach, near Polzeath.

Following page Beach paradise at Trebarwith strand, near Tintagel, a beautiful combination of sand, pools, caves and rocks.

Left Mother Ivey's bay, Trevose, a fine example of the purity of Cornwall's waters.

Right Enjoying the wind at Perran beach, north of Perranporth.

Cornwall's north coast, whilst essentially rocky, has many fine beaches of golden sand. Some, such as Widemouth, Sandy mouth, Booby's bay, Watergate, Perran, or St Ives bay have extensive stretches of sand, up to five miles in the case of St Ives. Others, such as Bossiney, Trebarwith, Crackington haven or Port Isaac are more intimate coves, often involving a scramble down a steep slope to reach them. The region to the west of St Ives is considerably more rugged, with granite rock and very few beaches. Even the most frequented beaches somehow retain a charm and innocence, qualities held by many other aspects of the county. Summer transforms this quiet backwater of England into a festival of holidaying humanity. Families are drawn here in their countless thousands to enjoy the sun and the pure water, to indulge for a short while in careless freedom. Whilst the sudden summer flood may invite resentment amongst the residents, in fact this invasion finances the nine months of the year when wild nature can be savoured in solitude.

surfing

North Cornwall is one of Europe's major destinations for surfers, those alternative, iconoclastic athletes who slide down waves. Particular combinations of exposure to wind and wave, slope of beach, currents and the compression of swelling water by rocky headlands make certain beaches highly desirable for the excitement of the surfing and for the associated scene of cafes and equipment shops. Polzeath, near Padstow, is a remarkable spectacle on a fine summer's day as the black of the wetsuits of thousands of surfers eclipses the blue of the sea. The two most popular regions are on the many beaches to be found north and south of Newquay and around Bude, although surfing is to be seen on almost every beach from Marsland to Sennen near Land's End.

Left Secluded surfing at Trevone bay.

Right Surfing in the sunset at Pentire.

Right Sea birds gliding the air of dusk near Trevone.

Top left Ocean kayaking at Porthcothan.

Bottom left Kayaking on the river Camel at Wadebridge.

Opposite top left Hand fishing in Padstow harbour.

Opposite top right Waterskiing at sunset in the Padstow estuary.

Opposite lower left Sailing in the Padstow estuary.

Opposite lower right Digging for fishing bait in Little Petheric creek.

outdoor fun

Many other water based activities are to be enjoyed in the clean rivers and sea around this coast; ocean kayaking, surf kayaking, river kayaking, fishing and sailing. The sheltered waters at the mouth of the Camel estuary at Padstow and inland towards Wadebridge are a particularly rich and popular playground for sailing and water skiing. The many scenic harbours and coves are the setting for endless family adventures messing about in boats.

Below Spectacular early light at Sandy mouth, north of Bude.

Opposite Shades of late evening near Trebarwith.

Above Ferns overhanging the Fowey river at Lanhydrock, Bodmin.

Above Fresh water meets the sea at Trevan

Above Ferns by the Camel river at Dunmere.

This page Summer garden flowers.
Following page Wild Montbretia.

Opposite, clockwise Sparrowhawk chick, kestrel, copper butterfly, red admiral butterfly, heath fritillary butterfly, dragonfly.

The former single track mineral railway, built to transport china clay from the processing plant at Wenford bridge to the port of Padstow, has now been transformed into a magnificent eighteen mile long car-free recreational trail for walkers, cyclists and horse riders. Each of the three stages has a different character. The section from Padstow to Wadebridge, which follows the Camel estuary, is open to wide views of water and hill and has a great richness of wayside flowers in the mild air next to the sea. The trail leaves Wadebridge to wander through lowland woodland of sycamore and beech, with the lazy waters of the Camel river meandering in the cow-grazed meadows. At Dunmere a short stretch of trail leads ahead to Bodmin town, whilst the main trail leads off left to follow the more wild upper parts of the river, more secretive and less frequented. This trail is one of the gems of Cornwall.

the camel trail

autumn

Autumn is full of the excitement of change in nature for the second time in the year, when the leaves of trees and shrubs and grasses begin to fade from shades of green to tints of red. At the same time the days start to sharpen towards frost and the scents of slowly decaying vegetation fill the clear air. This is a time of rich stimulation for the senses, a reminder of the simple beauty of being alive.

Opposite page Bracken flushed with the rich colours of autumn.

Following page The woodland around Golitha falls, to the south-east of Bodmin moor, is spectacular in the autumn.

Left Barnacle geese in the Camel estuary, a nature reserve which lies alongside the Camel trail from Wadebridge to Padstow.

Right Beech woodland surrounds the Camel river in the upper reaches of the Camel trail near Dunmere.

Opposite upper Granite buildings at Zennor, to the west of St Ives

Opposite lower left Carnival princesses at Tintagel.

Opposite lower right At Wenford bridge, the starting point for the Camel trail.

Above Lobster pots stacked in the harbour at Port Isaac.

Right Twisted old buildings in Port Isaac near the harbour.

A great deal of the charm of this corner of England lies in the romantic villages, constructed from local stone. The villages at the mouths of the many rivers flowing into the sea of the north coast of Cornwall have a ruggedly rich character based around the fishing which has traditionally been the livelihood of the residents. Little harbours sheltered by stone jetties protect the boats from the high storm seas and provide visitors with the flavour of a life more simple than that at home. The houses, usually reached by narrow lanes accessible only on foot, spread up the steep valley sides. Inland the villages are more expansive in the largely flat terrain of farmland, where a tractor may be seen outside the village pub. Those in the north of the county, such as St Teath, St Mabyn or Blisland have a cosy lightness, whereas the granite dwellings around Land's End are more stern. Summer brings the colourful joy of carnivals to many of the villages.

Above Sunset at Yeol mouth, near Morwenstow, looking towards the distant Hartland point in Devon.

Opposite Horses grazing the cliff top pastures bordering the wild stretch of coast north of Bude.

Following page Beech leaves in mid autumn, poised between summer and winter, in the woodlands around Golitha falls, south east of Bodmin moor.

Above St Ives harbour. This highly characterful town has an energy and a quality of light that has attracted artists for many decades, amongst them the famous sculptor, Barbara Hepworth. Their work may be seen in the scores of galleries hiding in the twisting streets.

Opposite page St Ives at night, seen from the northern end of St Ives bay at Godrevy point.

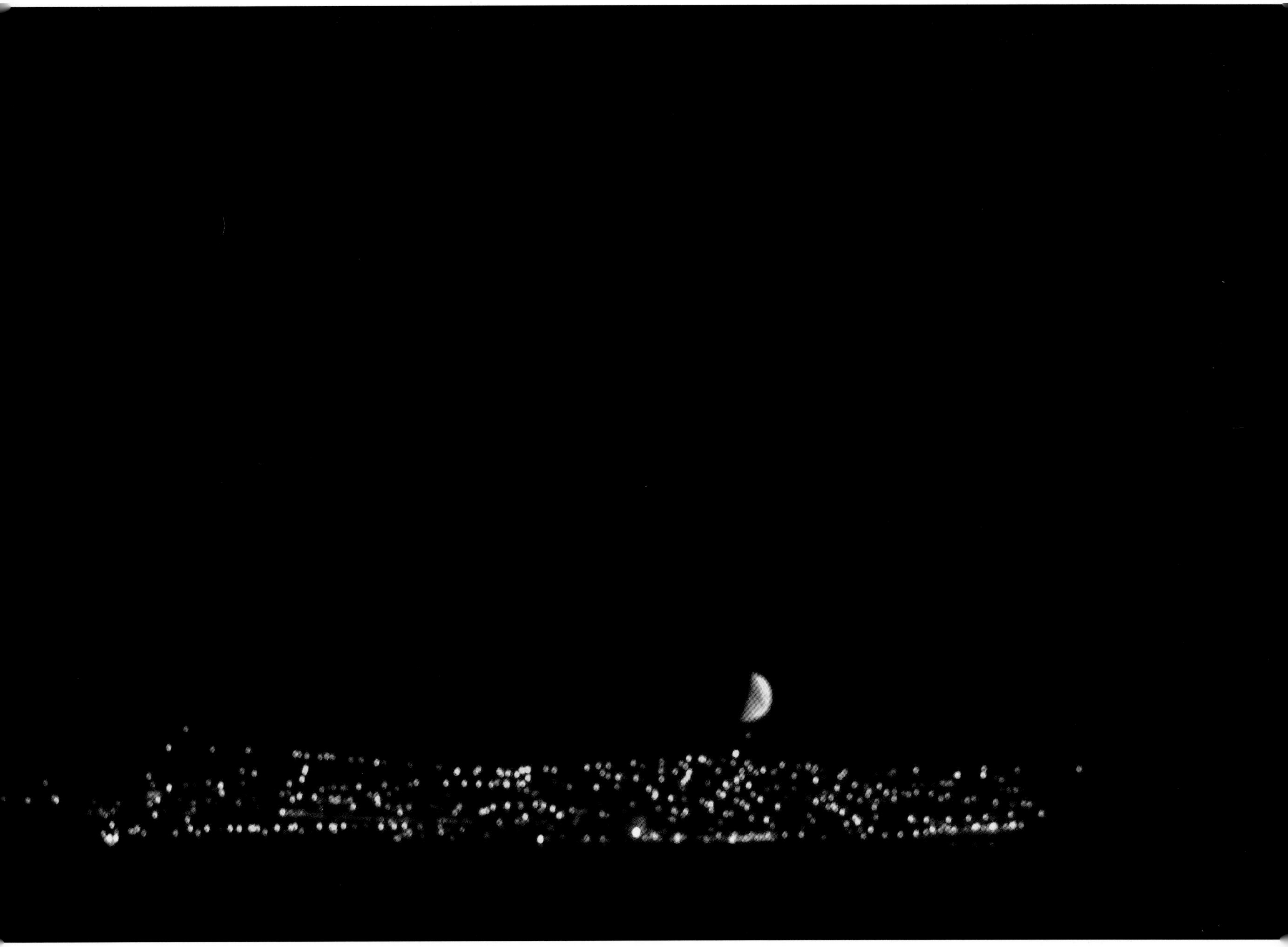

Above Bramble and bracken leaves stained with shades of autumn.

Opposite Honey fungus, one of the many species of fungus which raise their fruiting bodies in the damp woodland floor in September and October.

Left The weathered summit rocks of Stowe's hill to the north of Minions, Bodmin moor.

Below The famous Cheesewring stones perched above the rim of the quarry on Stowe's hill. The pile of stones to the right was added many years ago in fear that the tower would fall over.

The sea cliffs of Cornwall's north coast provide a powerful arena for the sport of rock climbing. The region of Penwith to the north of Penzance with its rough and solid granite rock, is perhaps the traditional area most notable for the quality and position of the climbing, with a large number of relatively easy but spectacular climbs; nearby, Sennen cove and Chair Ladder give many more fine climbs. More recently developed areas, such as the cliffs of Rumps point north of Polzeath, Tintagel head and the coast around Sharpnose point and many other smaller cliffs give extreme climbing on other types of rock. The mild climate and the situation of climbing above the rich blue of the sea, together with the mellow ambience of the culture of Cornwall, makes days spent climbing here into experiences that linger in the mind for a long time.

Left The third and last pitch of the superb but easy climb, Doorpost, at Bosigran.

Right The final moves on Doorpost, high above the blue of the ocean.

Following pages 108 and 109 The sun meeting rock and sea at the mouth of Boscastle harbour.

Following pages 110 and 111 The new moon hangs over the sea at Trevan point, near Polzeath.

index